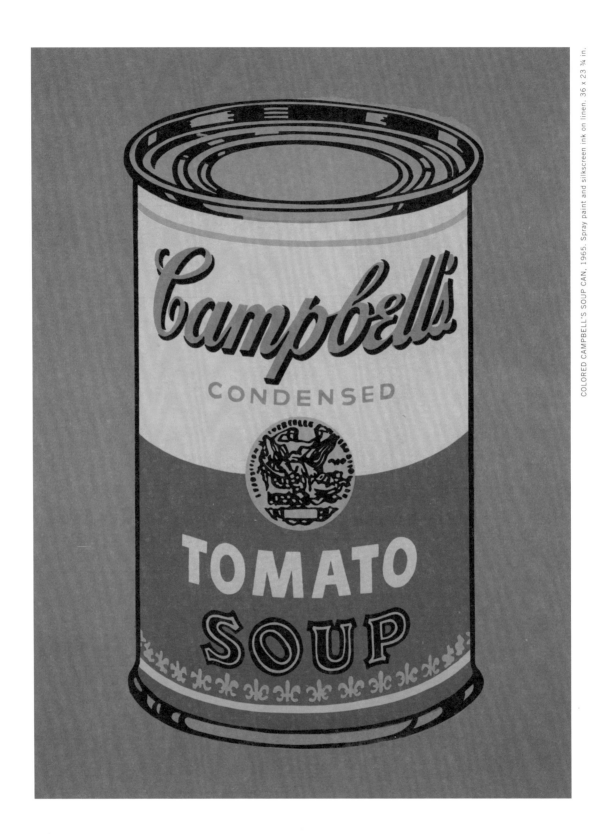

COLORED CAMPBELL'S SOUP CAN, 1965. Spray paint and silkscreen ink on linen. 36 x 23 ¾ in.

" POP ART IS FOR EVERYONE."

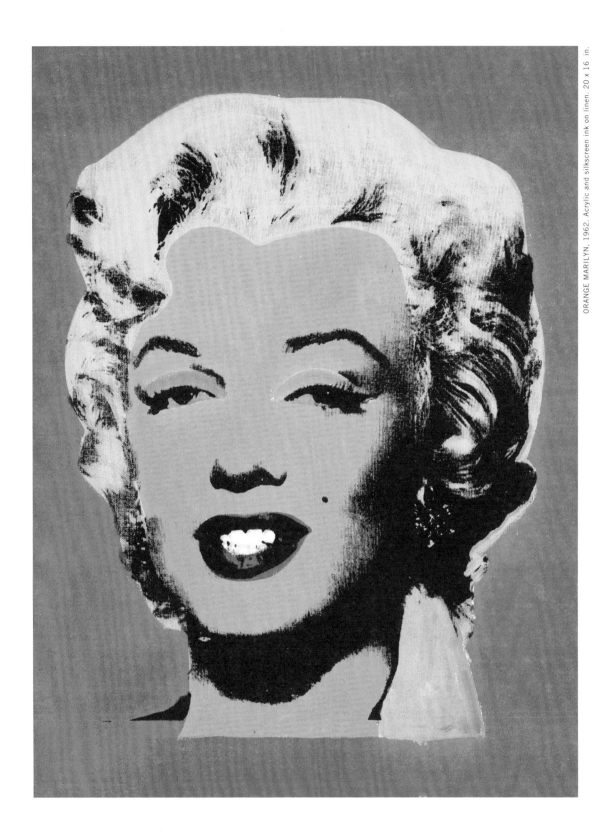

ORANGE MARILYN, 1962. Acrylic and silkscreen ink on linen. 20 x 16 in.

"MY NEW LINE IS: IN 15 MINUTES EVERYBODY WILL BE FAMOUS."

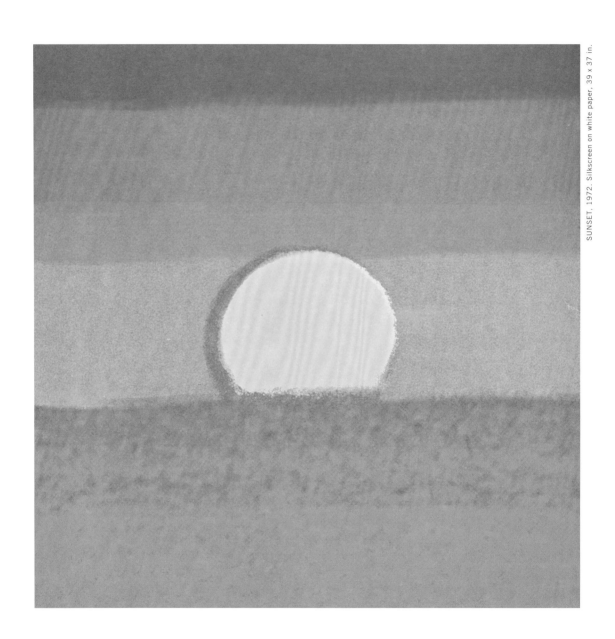

SUNSET, 1972. Silkscreen on white paper, 39 x 37 in.

"THE IDEA OF WAITING FOR SOMETHING MAKES IT MORE EXCITING."

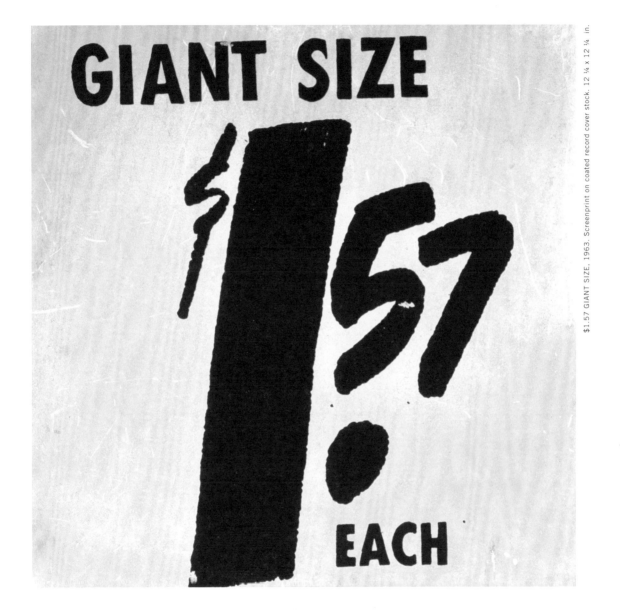

$1.57 GIANT SIZE, 1963. Screenprint on coated record cover stock. 12 ¼ x 12 ¼ in.

" WASTING MONEY PUTS YOU IN A REAL PARTY MOOD."

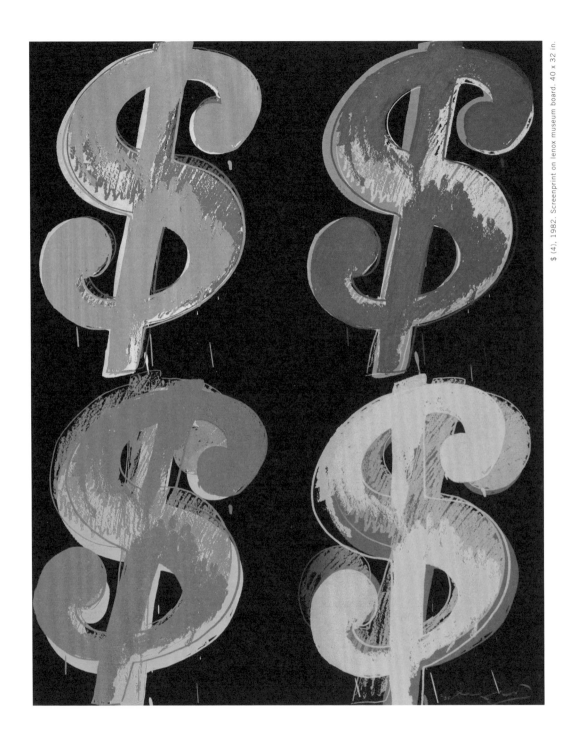

$ (4). 1982. Screenprint on lenox museum board. 40 x 32 in.

"BEING GOOD IN BUSINESS IS THE MOST FASCINATING KIND OF ART."

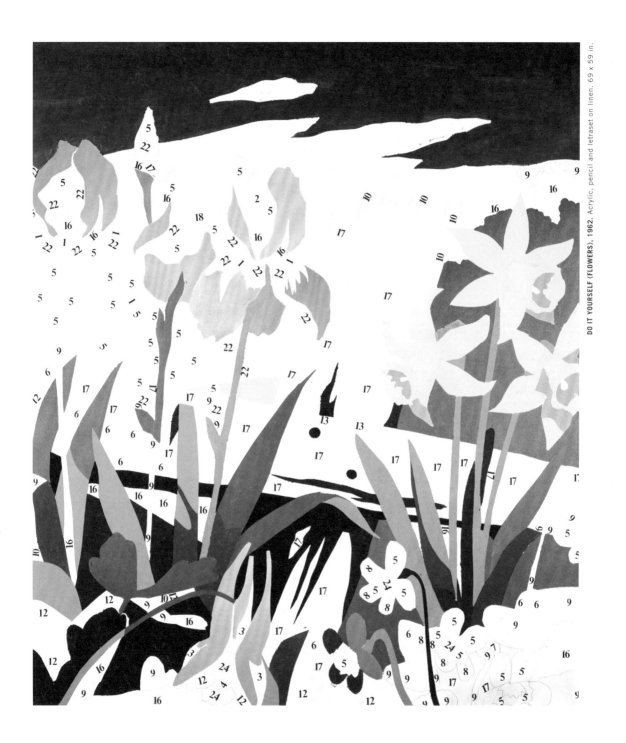

DO IT YOURSELF (FLOWERS), 1962. Acrylic, pencil and letraset on linen. 69 x 59 in.

"AND NOW WHAT PEOPLE WANT IS ONLY ONE OF A KIND."

"ALL IS PRETTY."

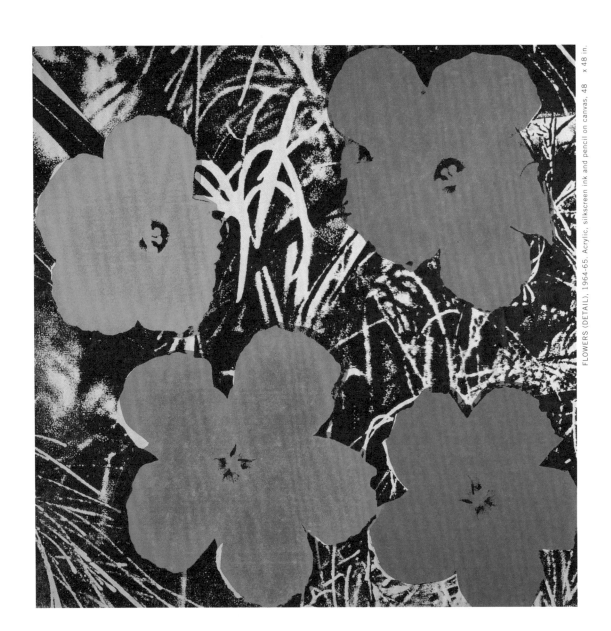

FLOWERS (DETAIL), 1964-65. Acrylic, silkscreen ink and pencil on canvas. 48   x 48 in.

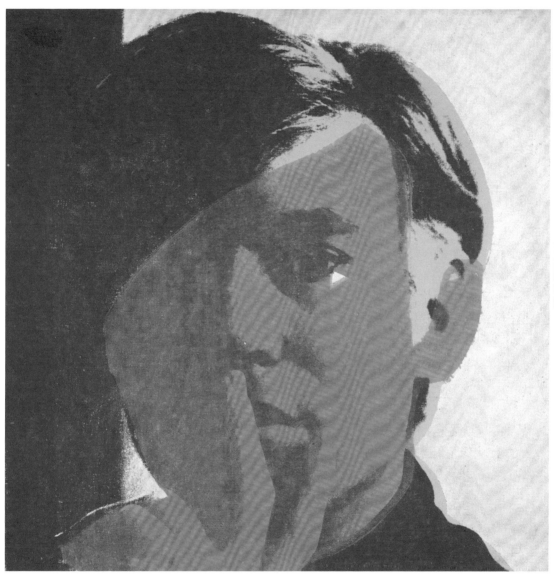

SELF-PORTRAIT (DETAIL), 1966. Acrylic and silkscreen ink on canvas.. 22 x 22 in.

"I THINK EVERYBODY SHOULD LIKE EVERYBODY."

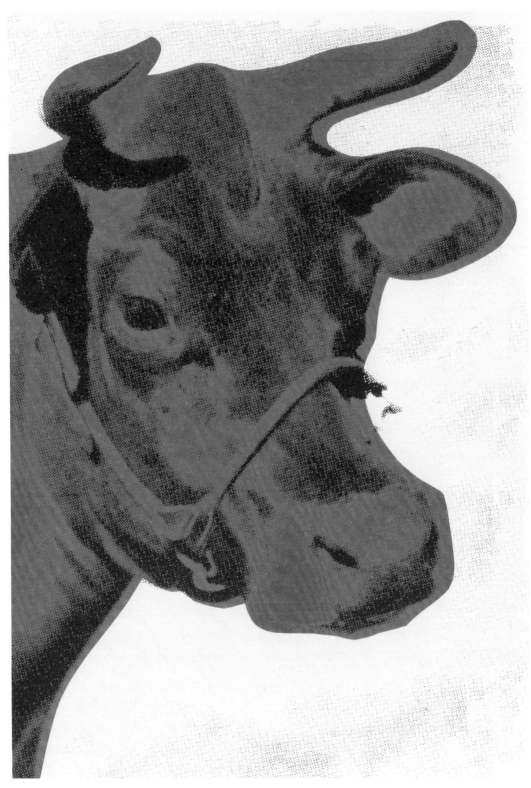

COW (DETAIL), 1966. Screenprint on wallpaper. 45 ½ x 29 ¾ in.

" IF EVERYBODY'S NOT A BEAUTY, THEN NOBODY IS."

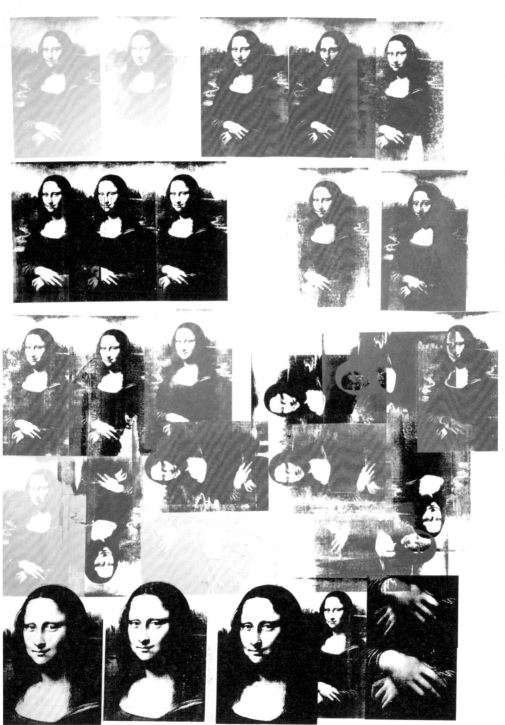

COLORED MONA LISA, 1963. Silkscreen ink and pencil on linen. 126 x 82 in.

"I DON'T KNOW WHERE THE ARTIFICIAL STOPS AND THE REAL STARTS."

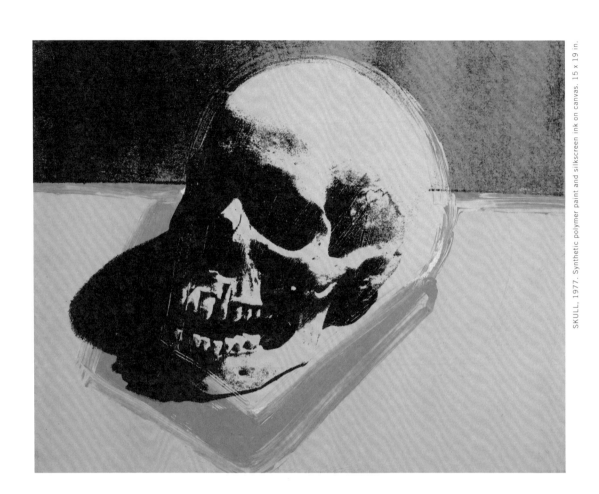

SKULL, 1977. Synthetic polymer paint and silkscreen ink on canvas. 15 x 19 in.

"THE WORLD FASCINATES ME."

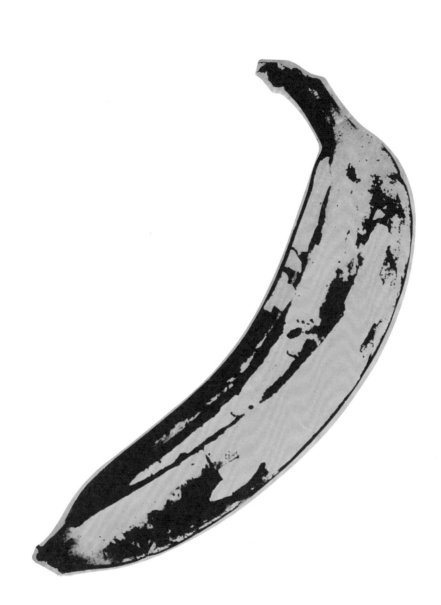

BANANA (DETAIL). 1966. Screenprint on styrene, 24 x 53 ¼ in.

" ART IS WHAT YOU CAN GET AWAY WITH."